Families and Cottaş
of
Old Birkdale and Ainsdale

edited by

Sylvia Harrop

Carnegie Publishing, 1992

This volume is dedicated to the memory of the late James F. Bradley who, with his friend Geoffrey Barnes, collected together so much information on local cottages.

Families and Cottages of Old Birkdale and Ainsdale

edited by Sylvia Harrop

Copyright, © Birkdale and Ainsdale Historical Research Society, 1992

Published by Carnegie Publishing Ltd., 18 Maynard Street, Preston, Lancashire, PR1 2AL
Typeset in 10/12 Times and Caslon Antique by Carnegie Publishing Ltd.
Printed and bound in the UK by T. Snape & Co. Ltd., Preston.

British Library Cataloguing-in-Publication Data
A CIP catalogue record for this book is available from the British Library

ISBN 0 948789 83 2

Contents

Introduction

THIS book can be read with enjoyment as it is, but to understand the background to life in the local farms, the reader is recommended to turn to my book *Old Birkdale and Ainsdale. Life on the south-west Lancashire Coast 1600–1851* (Birkdale and Ainsdale Historical Research Society, 1985 and 1986). This provides details on the lords of the manor, farming practices and everyday life in the two communities.

Until recent times, surnames were often spelt in several different ways. The most common example is Rimmer, which could appear as Rimmer, Rimer, Rymer or Rymmer. To avoid confusion, all names used in the accounts here have been standardised. Those in the family trees, however, are as found in the parish register. Words and terms commonly used in old Birkdale and Ainsdale, but not in regular use now, are listed in a glossary at the back.

Each account is illustrated by photographs, paintings or drawings, and by a family tree which refers to at least one of the families who lived in the cottage. The mills and cottages are described here as though a traveller were going from north to south, starting right on the North Meols/Birkdale boundary with Birkdale Mill, and ending with White House Farm, which actually straddles the boundary between Ainsdale and Formby. The site of each building is shown on the map across the centre pages, taken from the historical map of *Birkdale and Ainsdale, Past and Present* published by the Birkdale and Ainsdale Historical Research Society.

The two mills have been included not only because windmills hold a fascination of their own, but also because they played a most important part in the local economies.

Acknowledgements

MOST of the spadework for this volume has been done by Rene Merritt and Joan Diggle of the Birkdale and Ainsdale Historical Research Society. It is really their book. Other members of the society have assisted in many ways, especially Pat Perrins, by typing up the text and helping to put the book together; Peggy Ormrod, by preparing the historical map; and Harry Foster and his friend Alan Whittaker, by helping with illustrations.

We acknowledge with grateful thanks the assistance of the following: Mrs. Eileen Abram, Mr. James Blundell, Mr. J. W. Farr, Mrs. Gertrude Forshaw, Dr. Brian Garston; Mrs. Janet Jenkins and Miss Joan Tarbuck of Sefton Libraries; the late Mr. and Mrs. Kay, Mrs. Brenda Pearson; Miss Margaret Proctor and Mr. Neil Sayer of the Merseyside Record Office; Mrs. Jean Rivett, former Curator of the Botanic Gardens Museum, Southport; Mrs. Muriel Sibley; Miss Janet Smith of Liverpool City Libraries.

Architectural Note

THE oldest cottages in the area, such as The Cottage in Birkdale and White House Farm in Ainsdale, were cruck-built. The 'crucks' were massive, curved timbers which met at the top like the sides of a letter 'A'. They were the main support of the roof, and external walls were attached to them (see illustration). These cottages had outer walls of 'clamstaff and daub', thatch roofs, and were either single-storey or of two storeys. From the eighteenth century, brick began to be used for new cottages and barns, with either thatch or stone roofs. Some farms were of the 'longhouse' type, with farmhouse and farm buildings all under one roof; others, the majority, had the house and farm buildings separate. Windows were small, usually with sliding sashes and small rectangular panes (see *Old Birkdale and Ainsdale*, chapter six).

White House Farm, Ainsdale.

Key to Family Trees

ba.	....	baptised
m.	....	married
bu.	....	buried
s.	....	son
d.	....	daughter

F	....	Formby parish register
H	....	Halsall parish register
CC	......	Christ Church, Southport, parish register
O	....	Ormskirk parish register

All other parish register entries are North Meols (St. Cuthbert's, Churchtown).

Old Birkdale Mill, by W. G. Herdman.

Birkdale Mill and Mill Cottages

THERE is a certain attraction about windmills, and Birkdale Mill was no exception. The fact that it had previously operated on the Fylde, at Kirkham, before being shipped to Birkdale adds an interesting slant to its history. It was in the mid-eighteenth century that it was dismantled, packed up, ferried across the Ribble, and reassembled in Birkdale. Until then Ainsdale Mill, built on the boundary between Ainsdale and Birkdale, had to serve both areas.

The mill was built on a high point on the Birkdale side of the boundary with North Meols (later Southport), at what is now the corner of Mosley Street and Grove Street, where it collected the prevailing westerly winds. The sails and the main body of the mill were constructed of wood, and the base was made of bricks. (In those days timber was a precious commodity in these parts, not freely available as it is today. Perhaps that is one of the reasons why use was made of the Fylde mill.) It was called a post- or peg-mill, because of the wooden post with a wheel on the end which turned the mill into the wind.

Although researches do not tell the full story of the operators of the mill and the occupants of the cottages, there are fascinating glimpses of six families who were involved in their history, albeit sometimes briefly. It seems that the miller of Ainsdale, Joseph Bibby, came up to Birkdale to take over the new mill around 1750. Within a couple of years, however, he died, leaving a widow, Ellen (who outlived him for thirty years) and three children. One of these, also Ellen, married James Marshall, whose mother had been transported after his birth (see *Weathercock Farm*, p36).

It is said that the mill was brought from the Fylde by one William Shaw. He was working the Church-town Mill at that time, and members of his family followed him in his trade. By 1792 the Birkdale miller was John Shaw, almost certainly William's grandson; in that year he leased land by the mill on which to build a house. This lease instructed that a building of two bays be built either on three roods of land close to the mill, or on the Mill Brow adjoining it, the yearly rent being twenty shillings (with an additional forty shillings if not paid within ten days of the due date!). The cottage was duly erected across the road from the mill. It is interesting that even at that late date it was still built in vernacular style: low, with small windows

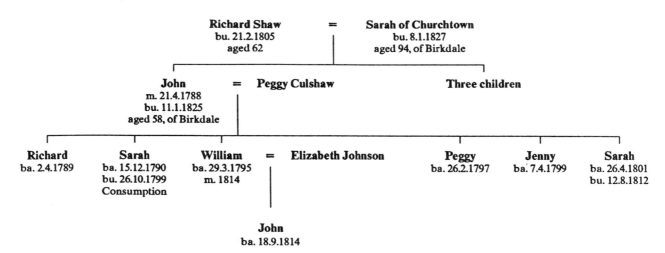

Richard Shaw
bu. 21.2.1805
aged 62

=

Sarah of Churchtown
bu. 8.1.1827
aged 94, of Birkdale

John
m. 21.4.1788
bu. 11.1.1825
aged 58, of Birkdale

=

Peggy Culshaw

Three children

Richard
ba. 2.4.1789

Sarah
ba. 15.12.1790
bu. 26.10.1799
Consumption

William
ba. 29.3.1795
m. 1814

=

Elizabeth Johnson

Peggy
ba. 26.2.1797

Jenny
ba. 7.4.1799

Sarah
ba. 26.4.1801
bu. 12.8.1812

John
ba. 18.9.1814

and a thatched roof.

Baptism records show that John and his family moved back to Churchtown within ten years, and a George Rainford is described as 'miller of Birkdale' in 1819. No-one seems to have held the post for long, possibly because the remuneration was low. Christopher Sutch was 'miller of Birkdale' when his daughter, Jane, was born in 1835, but he also disappears rather quickly from the records for, by 1841, his wife Ellen was living on Little Common with an infant son, and with no mention of her husband or their other two children.

Peter Travis was the miller in 1841 and resided at the Mill Cottage with his wife, Elizabeth, five children and mother-in-law, Hannah. It is tempting to think that Elizabeth could be the sister of Christopher Sutch, as the dates and names coincide so exactly and, if true, it would add another romantic touch to the mill story.

By 1851 the miller had changed yet again: Thomas

Rimmer, son of the blacksmith William Rimmer, now held the post and, for the only time on record, had an assistant, Charles Brocklebank. They both lived with William at his cottage just south of the mill. The Mill House was then occupied by Hugh Marshall, an agricultural labourer, and his extremely large family, who lived there until its demolition. The last time the house was recorded was in the census of 1871.

One wonders how John and William Shaw, George Rainford, Christopher Sutch and Thomas Rimmer reacted to the attentions of numerous visitors over the summer months, for their mill was one of the main tourist attractions for visitors to the fast-developing new town of Southport. Scores of middle-class ladies, in particular, taught to draw and paint as a necessary accomplishment, found the mill a delightful subject for their talents, and an agreeable means of using up their long holidays in the town. Others just walked over from Southport to see the quaint mill and its group of cottages, and to look at the view from Mill Brow.

By the middle of the nineteenth century, however, the mill's days were numbered. The development of 'new' Birkdale began in the first years of the 1850s, and Grove Street and Upper Aughton Road were laid out and built up very early. Hugh Marshall was the last incumbent of the Mill House, and the last miller

Old Ned's Mill, Birkdale, by H. Backhouse.

recorded was Thomas Parkinson from Liverpool in 1861. An account by W. Hodge in the *Southport Visiter* around 1906 reported: 'The windmill situated in Mill Lane was pulled down in the eighteen-sixties and with that an old landmark was gone. Hugh Marshall's house followed in the eighteen-eighties and then that of Thomas Rimmer, who was well known as a band conductor.'

After little more than a century, the building that proved Birkdale's most popular attraction was gone.

The Cottage at the beginning of this century.

The Cottage, 74 Liverpool Road, Birkdale

THROUGHOUT its long history the Cottage, or as it has been variously known, Rimmers, Carrs, or The Cab Cottage, has been a landmark for travellers passing through Birkdale. Access to the Cottage was originally from North Side Lane, a sandy track skirting the sandhills and fields, and joining Mill Lane to the north and Wham Lane to the south. The lane evolved into a road (Liverpool Road), the area was developed, and all the other farm cottages were demolished leaving this, the only survivor in Birkdale of a building recognisable as a typical local farmhouse. In 1970, when houses were built immediately behind the property, its rural aspect was lost, but its unique character remains.

It is difficult to date precisely a cruck-built house such as this without documentary evidence. Throughout the Middle Ages and well into the eighteenth century yeoman farmers' cottages were constructed in a similar way, with massive rough-hewn timbers giving the main support to the roof, and with the external walls attached to them. The outside walls of this cottage consist of wooden posts (clamstaff) plastered with daub, while the inner ones are constructed of the slightly less substantial wattle and daub, and the roof is thatched. In 1974 much replastering had to be done after the cottage was vandalised, but the basic structure remains intact.

This is a three-bay cottage, the central one forming the firehouse, open to the rafters and containing the fireplace and the front door. At each end the house has two storeys, the rooms being very low-ceilinged and the doors less than five feet high, with handmade leather hinges. Originally the room at the north end downstairs was divided, to provide a stone-shelved buttery at the front and a sleeping area at the back. In the wall at the south end was a bread oven. Access to the upper rooms in the early days was by ladder. The floors were of earth covered with flagstones, which were sanded and swept. It is reported that a bucket of sand, kept handy for the purpose, was used to good

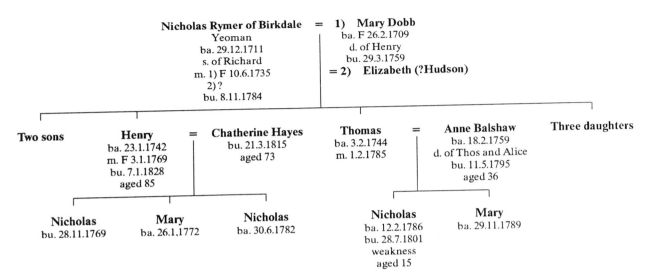

Nicholas Rymer of Birkdale = 1) Mary Dobb
Yeoman / ba. F 26.2.1709 / d. of Henry / bu. 29.3.1759
ba. 29.12.1711
s. of Richard
m. 1) F 10.6.1735
2) ?
bu. 8.11.1784
= 2) Elizabeth (?Hudson)

Two sons

Henry = **Chatherine Hayes**
ba. 23.1.1742 / bu. 21.3.1815 / aged 73
m. F 3.1.1769
bu. 7.1.1828
aged 85

Thomas = **Anne Balshaw**
ba. 3.2.1744 / ba. 18.2.1759 / d. of Thos and Alice / bu. 11.5.1795 / aged 36
m. 1.2.1785

Three daughters

Nicholas
bu. 28.11.1769

Mary
ba. 26.1,1772

Nicholas
ba. 30.6.1782

Nicholas
ba. 12.2.1786 / bu. 28.7.1801 / weakness / aged 15

Mary
ba. 29.11.1789

effect to fight a fire in the chimney on at least one occasion.

Outside there was a barn built at right angles to the house along what is now Crosby Road, and there was a well in front of the cottage door. Close by, to the east, was North Side Lane Cottage, and beyond that was North End House.

The survival of this cottage must owe much to the families of Rimmers, and their close relatives the Carrs, who are thought to have been the occupants for much of its history. Certainly in 1809 Nicholas Rimmer held the lease of the property, which was being farmed by Thomas and Henry Rimmer. They had nearly seventeen acres of land, most of which was arable and pasture around the farmhouse. The remainder was meadowland along the boundary with Halsall: just under an acre on the Wham and a strip of a third of an acre on the Gorstile. Shares of these good meadows were very important to farms whose fields were on sandy soil reclaimed from the dunes, and it is very interesting that there was a system in Birkdale by which good land was shared out.

Towards the end of the nineteenth century there was a flourishing dairy at the Cottage and James Rimmer (son of another Nicholas) was living there, acting as dairyman farmer for his cousin, Elizabeth Carr. In 1891 he married Catherine Kirby at St. Peter's Church, and after the turn of the century he became a 'cabby'. He and his wife, who was a nurse, were well-known in the locality, as she wore a rather quaint uniform which included a distinctive bonnet and neck ruffle, and he wore a shiny top hat on occasions when driving his hansom cab. James died in 1936, but his son James carried on the business until his death in 1972.

Catherine strove to keep the historic features of the cottage intact, even to the extent of denying herself the comforts of mains water and gas or electricity when they became available. Paradoxically, the Cottage was on the telephone from the early days of the National Telephone Company, because of the needs of the hackney cab and taxi business, and for Catherine's nursing service.

The Cottage in 1970, by Muriel Sibley.

When the Cottage was vacated in 1972 and was empty for some years, its future was very much in doubt. Fortunately, it has survived, and is listed as a building of historic interest by the Department of the Environment. It is certainly an irreplaceable piece of the history of Birkdale.

Ash Tree Inn, by E. Beattie, 1875.

8

The Ash Tree Inn and Farm, Birkdale

SOME of the older generation in Birkdale still refer to 'Th' owd Ash'. This is an affectionate reference to the little eighteenth-century hostelry, the Ash Tree Inn, which once stood near the junction of the present Kew Road and Bedford Road. The site is now occupied by the Portland Hotel, and although the small white-washed building vanished one hundred years ago, its name still clings to its Victorian successor.

The builder of the Ash Tree Inn was Thomas, the enterprising son of a Birkdale yeoman, James Rimmer. Their farmhouse stood amid its sandy fields on the north side of the present Bedford Road, opposite the Portland Hotel. Inn-keeping may have been in the family: a 'Thomas Rymer landlord' is recorded in 1737, and James' eldest son, Robert, became a landlord in Formby. His career was brief, however, as he died in 1761 at the age of only thirty, leaving one child, Isabel. Yeoman James co-operated in the building project, but died whilst the new inn was being built in the year 1774. He left most of his property between his son, Thomas, and daughter, Mary, the wife of Richard Carr. Mary received some luxurious items by the standards of the day, including six silver teaspoons, 'cheane' (presumably china), pewter, and a corner cupboard. The Carrs then lived in Blowick, but a family arrangement seems to have been made by which Mary and Richard took over the farmhouse, and Thomas, newly married to Richard's sister, Margaret Carr, moved into his new brick-built house. Thomas' share of the holding seems to have been mainly rough ground: seven acres described as warren; just over three acres called Ash Tree hey; and a small area described as 'building and garden'.

The house was in an advantageous position close to the junction of two ancient trackways, one leading to Scarisbrick and the south-east, and the other a route across marshland, called Wham Lane. Thomas was still a husbandman, but his inn became increasingly important and lucrative as the town of Southport developed. Visitors found an excursion to the Isle of Wight, as the district was named (or nicknamed), a pleasant change. They would drive out in donkey carriages, drawn by up to three donkeys, which coped better than horses with the sandy terrain. A writer in the nineteenth century stated: 'There is a little inn and in the season it is no uncommon thing to see thirty or

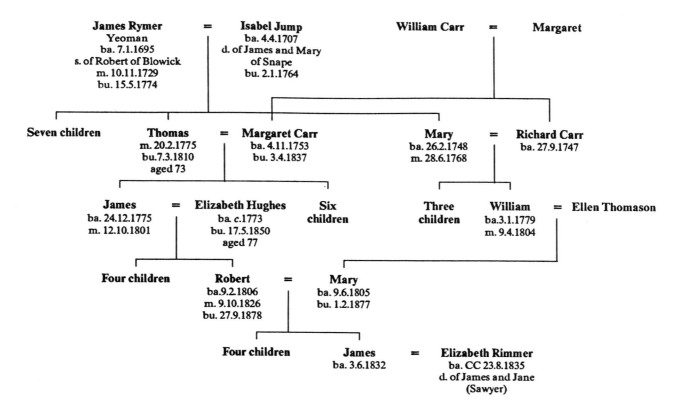

James Rymer
Yeoman
ba. 7.1.1695
s. of Robert of Blowick
m. 10.11.1729
bu. 15.5.1774

=

Isabel Jump
ba. 4.4.1707
d. of James and Mary
of Snape
bu. 2.1.1764

William Carr = Margaret

Seven children

Thomas
m. 20.2.1775
bu.7.3.1810
aged 73

=

Margaret Carr
ba. 4.11.1753
bu. 3.4.1837

Mary
ba. 26.2.1748
m. 28.6.1768

=

Richard Carr
ba. 27.9.1747

James
ba. 24.12.1775
m. 12.10.1801

=

Elizabeth Hughes
ba. c.1773
bu. 17.5.1850
aged 77

Six
children

Three
children

William
ba.3.1.1779
m. 9.4.1804

=

Ellen Thomason

Four children

Robert
ba.9.2.1806
m. 9.10.1826
bu. 27.9.1878

=

Mary
ba. 9.6.1805
bu. 1.2.1877

Four children

James
ba. 3.6.1832

=

Elizabeth Rimmer
ba. CC 23.8.1835
d. of James and Jane
(Sawyer)

forty donkeys and a dozen or twenty donkey carriages tethered in front of the hotel'. Thomas had leased land in front of his inn, and there he laid out a bowling green for his patrons. The more energetic could also enjoy a scramble up to the flagpole which marked the highest point of the adjacent sandhills. This vantage point gave good views over the surrounding countryside: Halsall Church and, beyond it, Clieves Hills and the rising ground towards Aughton could be seen. Further away, Parbold and Ashurst Beacon and the stone tower mill on Harrock Hill would be visible, and on really clear days the Pennines and the hills of Lakeland.

At certain times of the year the gipsies would arrive and set up an encampment, which provided another novelty for the visitors. They could also regale themselves on bacon and eggs and other rural refreshments, perhaps in the shade of the tree which gave both the inn and the neighbouring farm their names.

Besides catering for the tourists, the Ash Tree Inn became an important meeting place for the community, housing events such as the meetings of local societies and their annual roast beef dinners. A notable event took place in 1845, when the implementation of the 1836 Tithe Commutation Act at last began in Birkdale. The landlord by that time was Thomas'

son James, aged seventy, and it must have been an important day for him when the lawyers representing the Lord of the Manor and the Rector of North Meols arrived at the inn to meet the Rector himself and the assistant Tithe Commissioner. Their task was to estimate the cash value of the tithes, which from time immemorial had been paid in kind. Perhaps the good fare provided by James assisted in the amicable outcome of their discussions.

James was still landlord in 1851, but by 1861 his second son, Robert, had taken over. Robert had previously farmed eight acres in North Side Lane, near the surviving cottage in Liverpool Road which in 1845 was occupied by Thomas Carr, a kinsman of Robert and of the Carrs of Ash Tree Farm. Sometime during the 1870s the ownership of the inn passed to a brewery. Robert's address was Upper Aughton Road when he died in 1878, a year after his wife Mary (Carr). He was quite prosperous, leaving bequests totalling £1,500 and leasehold property in Stamford Road, and having acquired the status of 'gentleman' according to the description in his will.

By 1881, the landlord of the Ash Tree was Robert Tilley, a 'foreigner' from Much Wenlock in Shropshire. Within the following decade civilisation set in, and the homely little building was superseded by the somewhat pretentious Portland Hotel, which must

Portland Hotel, Bedford Road.

have looked strangely out of place among the sandy wastes which were still nearby. Landlord Thomas would perhaps have been pleased to know that not far from his bowling green another form of healthy recreation had begun. In 1889 the newly-formed Birkdale Golf Club secured land for a golf course adjacent to Bedford Road and Liverpool Road, and reserved rooms at the Portland Hotel to serve as its headquarters. Part of the course lay across what is now Bedford Park, and this was the cradle for the first eight years of the now famous Royal Birkdale Golf Club, until its transfer to the Hillside dunes.

Shaw's House, Birkdale

ON Shaws Road, just off what used to be Birkdale Common, stands a modern house, incorporating all that remains of the old Shaw's House and farm. Its name, unchanged since the early eighteenth century, derives from a Downholland family which occupied the property for a comparatively brief period of its history. Before 1720 it was known as 'Birches', from an old Birkdale family which was already established in the township when parish records began at the end of the sixteenth century.

In August 1674 Ellin Birch married Gorgue (George) Shaw of Downholland at Halsall Church. She was the only surviving child of James Birch, and when he died in 1685 she and George took over the family farm. It was a substantial farm: in addition to land on the sandy soil of Birkdale, George and Ellin leased part of Birkdale Moss, just over the brook in Halsall parish. On a list of those liable for 'Prescription Money for tythe Hay within Halsall due to the Rector of Halsall from Inhabitants in Birkdell' in 1720, George Shaw paid by far the largest sum, 13s. 4d., for Birches. The next highest was less than half this, 6s. owed by James Jump, and only two of the remaining fourteen people listed paid more

than a shilling.

George Shaw died in 1724, in his seventies. Ellin had died long before, in 1685, predeceasing two of their three children. Only one, Edward, survived childhood. When, in 1725, the lease on the family farm was renewed, 'adding two lives to one in being', the three lives named were those of Edward and two of his sons, George and James. Despite farming in Birkdale, however, the family does not appear at all in the North Meols parish registers. All their baptisms, marriages and funerals are at Halsall, and they are still described as 'of Downholland'. Presumably they occupied Birches until about 1755, for an endorsement on the 1725 lease states:

Nov 18th 1755 . . . I Richard Brettargh Steward then received from Edward Segar Ten guineas a full year value for the estate in Birkdale late George Shaw's being paid by him the said Ed. Segar for tenant rights for the said Estate and I do admit him tenant thereof . . . to hold to him his heirs and assigns according as it hath or might have done to the within named Edward Shaw . . . etc.

Edward Segar had to pay for taking over the tenancy

Shaw's House in 1974.

14

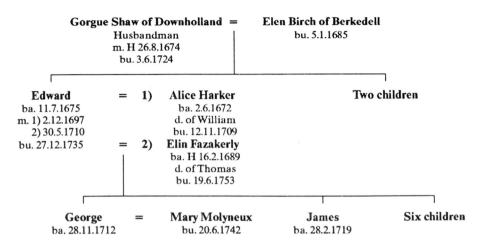

Gorgue Shaw of Downholland = **Elen Birch of Berkedell**
Husbandman   bu. 5.1.1685
m. H 26.8.1674
bu. 3.6.1724

Edward = 1)   **Alice Harker**   **Two children**
ba. 11.7.1675   ba. 2.6.1672
m. 1) 2.12.1697   d. of William
2) 30.5.1710   bu. 12.11.1709
bu. 27.12.1735 = 2)   **Elin Fazakerly**
ba. H 16.2.1689
d. of Thomas
bu. 19.6.1753

George = **Mary Molyneux**   **James**   **Six children**
ba. 28.11.1712   bu. 20.6.1742   ba. 28.2.1719

nearly five times the annual rent required in the 1725 lease. It was then 22s. 8d. paid twice yearly at Pentecost and St. Martin, plus 'one wether sheep annually, one cow every second year, one day's shearing, boons and services as accustomed and rabbits 3s.'.

The new lease gives a description of the property in 1725: '. . . firehouse three bays. Outhousing six bays land where the house stands Commonly called the new ground ten acres. Half of New Hey in Birkdale one acre. Total 11 acres. A fishing stall at sea'. Shaw's house was, therefore, then a three-bay farmhouse, with six bays of barn and outbuildings standing in ten acres, and it held the very valuable lease of a fishing stall on the shore. It was not the Birkdale lands, however, that mattered to the new owner, who sold the fishing stall to Thomas Aindow. Edward Segar was more interested in the land leased with the farm on Birkdale Moss.

The Segars must have known the Shaw family well, for they had been near neighbours in the Barton and Downholland areas of Halsall for many decades. Edward Segar, of Barton House, was described as a

Albert Dutton, Snr., with his cattle in Shaftesbury Road in the 1930s.

'gentleman' and numbered among his ancestors a rector, curates, school-master and parish clerk of Halsall. His great achievement was the first successful draining of the mossland to the west of Halsall. It was in the 1750s, just when he took the lease on Shaw's House, that he began the long task of reclaiming his mossland, and it seems likely that he began on Birkdale Moss. He died in 1768 before the process was complete, and left his Shaw's estate in two halves: one half to his eldest son, John, and the other to his grandson Edward. (His third son, William, had renewed a lease on a farm in Ainsdale in 1760 and founded the Segars of Ainsdale.) By 1809, however, the Segars had left Shaw's House, as James Livesley was farming the land.

James came to Birkdale from Formby, where his family had lived since records began in 1620. In 1790 he married Jenny Sutton of Common End Farm, and they were 'of Birkdale' when their son Thomas was baptised at Formby in 1801. James and Jenny Livesley appear to have had only three children, two of whom survived, but their son Thomas married at eighteen and had three sons and two daughters who, between them, provided James with at least twelve great-grandchildren, eight of whom were born in his lifetime. He was alive, aged 89, at the date of the 1851 census, but had died before 1861. As the family expanded, new leases were negotiated and in 1845 there were two Livesley farms, next to one another. Thomas farmed Shaw's House with 71 acres, including 39 acres of warren, and his son Miles farmed 51 acres, mainly on Charnleys Hills, with his wife Elizabeth, daughter of Miles and Margery Blundell of Charnleys and South End Farm. Old James was then living in Aughton's House, at the north end of the Common (between what is now Clifford Road and Shaws Road) with a small garden, surrounded by his son Thomas's lands.

By 1861 changes had taken place: old James was dead, and Thomas had moved to Aughton's House. He shared this farm with Henry Marshall, who was probably his son-in-law, and they farmed twelve and 23 acres respectively. Shaw's House was now occupied by Thomas Marshall and his wife Margery Tomlinson, who had come from a farm at Hillside. They and their descendants were the last in the long line of farmers at Shaw's House. Thomas, however, was also a builder and was thus involved in the creation of new Birkdale: he is believed to have financed the row of semi-detached houses at the corner of Shaws Road and Shaftesbury Road.

Township Cottages today.

18

Township Cottages, Birkdale

THE quaint cottages still standing in Sandon Road, contrasting so sharply with their surroundings, give no hint of the part they played in the history of Birkdale. Sometime in the eighteenth century the township of Birkdale had built this row of cottages, then comprising four tiny dwellings with brick walls and thatched roofs, to house its needy poor. There is no record of their condition before 1814, but by then the recipients of the help were living in the utmost squalor. They had literally just a roof over their heads, and that of minute proportions, sometimes leaking through the thatch. Families of up to nine in number lived in this space, which comprised a living room of four yards by three and a sleeping area of four yards by two. Within the walls, blackened by smoky chimneys and with windows broken, the floors were mostly earthen, with a few bricks begged from the township's Poor Relief Fund to form some makeshift hearth or oven.

Following the report of 1814, giving such a graphic account of the situation, a sum of £3 17s. 0d. was spent on repairs to the cottages. It was a time of rapidly increasing calls upon the township for help, but another twenty years passed before the 'New Poor Law', as it was called, was introduced. Local Guardians of the Poor were elected in each parish, working through a Union, Birkdale being part of the Formby Union and nine such Unions being centred at Ormskirk. There was no longer any function, therefore, for the 'Town's Cottages for the Poor', as they had been called, and they were sold off. In 1840 Mary Rimmer owned them, since she left them in her will to her children. The new private owner, Mary or her predecessor, had made the cottages more habitable by converting the original four into two; and they have remained as such ever since, though with extensions and modernisation. Their connection with the unions was brief, but the name 'Union Cottages' clung to them for many years – for example, in the census returns of 1861 and 1871.

In 1814 those unfortunate souls obliged to accept the meagre housing available were listed in the report. The first named was William Roughley, the illegitimate son of William Roughley and Ellen Aughton, who was born on the 13th June 1781, and married in 1802 to Jennet Meadows. They and their five children lived in one cottage, and no doubt their other two children born after 1814 also. William was a day

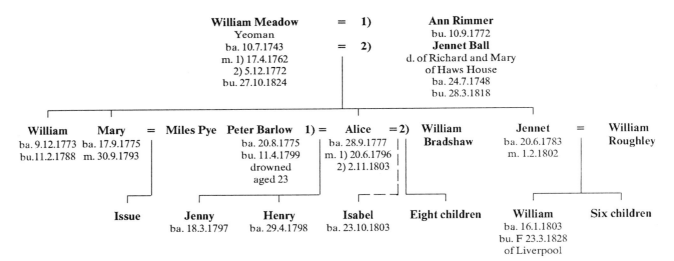

William Meadow   = 1)   **Ann Rimmer**
Yeoman   bu. 10.9.1772
ba. 10.7.1743   = 2)   **Jennet Ball**
m. 1) 17.4.1762   d. of Richard and Mary
2) 5.12.1772   of Haws House
bu. 27.10.1824   ba. 24.7.1748
                              bu. 28.3.1818

William   **Mary** = **Miles Pye**   **Peter Barlow** 1) = **Alice** = 2) **William**   **Jennet** = **William**
ba. 9.12.1773   ba. 17.9.1775   ba. 20.8.1775   ba. 28.9.1777   **Bradshaw**   ba. 20.6.1783   **Roughley**
bu.11.2.1788   m. 30.9.1793   bu. 11.4.1799   m. 1) 20.6.1796   m. 1.2.1802
                             drowned   2) 2.11.1803
                             aged 23

             Issue   **Jenny**   **Henry**   **Isabel**   **Eight children**   **William**   **Six children**
                      ba. 18.3.1797   ba. 29.4.1798   ba. 23.10.1803   ba. 16.1.1803
                                                bu. F 23.3.1828
                                                of Liverpool

labourer, or casual labourer: these, unlike regular workers, could not join a friendly society to see them through hard times, and they found themselves, together with the widowed, sick and elderly, amongst the poorest in the community.

William's wife, Jennet, had a sister, Alice, who was also living at one of the cottages with her husband William Bradshaw and seven children. Alice had suffered extraordinary tragedy in her life before she married William. She had been married to Peter Barlow who, on the 11th April 1799, went out fishing with three sons of William and Betty Hodges. All four perished at sea, and at the age of 22 Alice was left with two young children. In 1803 she had an illegitimate child, Isabel, and shortly afterwards married its father, William Bradshaw, by whom she had another eight children. Several died as infants, one being named Richard on the day that his five-year-old brother Richard was buried. This same Richard emerged again in the story in 1851 and thereafter, as an occupant of Union Cottages for the latter part of the nineteenth century.

20

Richard and his generation of Bradshaws started a series of family connections with another recurring name at Union Cottages, that of the Balls. Richard married Alice Ball, daughter of James Ball, who was resident there in 1841, while his brother William and sister Mary also married into other branches of the Ball family. By 1851 James Ball was widowed and living with Richard and Alice and their children, continuing to do so throughout the 'sixties and 'seventies. Another James Ball was also living with them, who was called a stepson of the Bradshaws, so the Balls and Bradshaws were well represented at the cottages throughout the years.

Having passed naturally from Bradshaws to Balls through their intermarriages, another of the original cottage-dwellers becomes linked into the chain that seems to tie nearly all the families together. The wife of James Ball (Richard Bradshaw's mother-in-law) was Margaret Rimmer, whose own mother, Margaret, herself lived in a Cottage for the Poor in 1814, with another old lady, Nancy Ball. It remains a mystery why the Rimmers and Carrs of the Ash Tree could not have supported her – and unusual, for the elderly stayed within the family unit as a rule.

By another strange coincidence, in 1834 the first elected Guardian of the Poor for Birkdale was John Pye, a well-to-do man of property. His mother was a sister of Jennet, wife of William Roughley, and also sister of Alice, wife of William Bradshaw, both of whom lived in the Cottages for the Poor in 1814. Their lives must have taken very differing paths.

Twentieth-century residents of the cottages remember the well, which used to be about three yards in front of the buildings. The privies, of the one-hole sentry-box type, were a good walk away, some twenty to thirty feet down the gardens at the back. It seems amazing that the Union Cottages have survived in spite of their history, and happily have seen much better days than those of their early years.

Sutton's Farm in the 1890s.

22

Sutton's or Common End Farm, Birkdale

IMAGINE a cosy farmhouse kitchen, stone-flagged floor covered with rugs, cheerful firelight reflected from a fine collection of gleaming copper and brass utensils on a shelf near the fireplace, a tall grandfather clock ticking away at the foot of the open staircase. This is the memory of Sutton's Farm still vividly recalled by a frequent visitor there in the first decade of this century.

The farmhouse stood in what is now Arundel Road, near to its junction with Dunbar Road. Its land extended to Sandon Road, of which there was a clear view from the house, with a footpath across the farm fields to the road. On the south side the land extended behind the Crown Hotel. In front of the house was a flower garden, and the big farmyard contained barns, shippons, a hen-house, and other buildings which housed cattle, horses, carts and farming gear. There was also a pond.

The barn (in the photograph overleaf) was near the house, the small building at the end being a wash-house. The dog kennel, in the early 1900s, was occupied by a wire-haired terrier of unpleasant disposition, necessary as a guard against the gipsies who appeared every August and, without permission, set up camp in the farm fields bordering Sandon Road. They helped themselves to the crops growing in the fields, which were principally peas, beans, potatoes, cabbages and turnips. These were grown to supply the Liverpool market and were taken there by horse and cart – the journey starting at 4 o'clock in the morning.

The photograph opposite shows the farmhouse with its open door revealing the whitewashed screen, or 'speer', which protected the fireplace from the draught. Coats were often hung on it, and this can be seen in the picture. Between the two windows a portion of the ceiling had been cut away to accommodate the height of the long-case clock. Against the far wall stood a settle, and folded back against the wall was a table, which was lowered at mealtimes and was large enough for a sizeable family – seven could sit comfortably around it.

The window on the right of the picture is that of the parlour, which housed the piano. The connecting wooden door was tarred black. The water supply was from a well close to the house, and the pump which raised the water can be seen on the extreme right of the picture. A drink of the sweet well-water was one of the pleasures enjoyed by the young visitors; another was the journey to and from home in the farm's horse-drawn cart. They also liked to watch the daughter of the house brushing her hair, which was exceptionally long and luxuriant. After brushing, it was polished with a silk handkerchief, and worn parted in the middle with an enormous bun on top.

Because of its situation at the southern end of Birkdale Common, the farm was also known as Common End Farm, and the first Sutton to farm and possibly to have built it, was James, an Ainsdale man.

James married Ellen Shorlicker in 1758. She was the eldest daughter of a well-known local couple, Robert and his wife 'Easter', or Esther, who were itinerant dealers in rabbit skins and who both lived to a great age. James and Ellen raised a family of seven, five daughters and two sons. The latter, Robert and James, remained unmarried. The youngest child, Jane, married William Rimmer of Birkdale in 1802 and it was her eldest son, Richard, who was living at the farm with his uncle, Robert Sutton, in the census of 1841. Uncle James lived with another relative, his niece Ellen and her husband John Pye, but evidently she displeased him, as he removed from their house before 1851 and left her, very pointedly, only one

Old Barn at Sutton's.

shilling in his will of 1855.

Robert and James had evidently prospered, for their wills refer to land and cottages in Scarisbrick. Both left bequests to all their nephews and nieces and to their surviving sisters, but it was Richard Rimmer who inherited Sutton's Farm, and there he and his wife Priscilla (Sawyer) raised their family of five sons and three daughters. Their second daughter, Margaret, married John Marshall, whose family lived at Meadow's Farm, Birkdale. It was Margaret who was

24

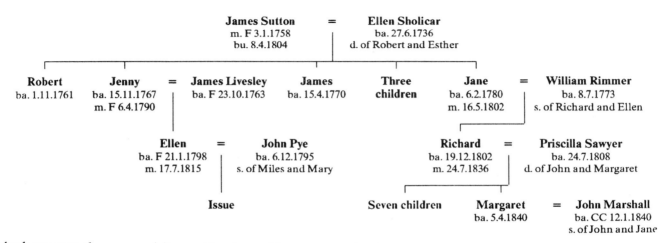

James Sutton = Ellen Sholicar
m. F 3.1.1758
bu. 8.4.1804
ba. 27.6.1736
d. of Robert and Esther

Robert
ba. 1.11.1761

Jenny = James Livesley
ba. 15.11.1767
m. F 6.4.1790
ba. F 23.10.1763

James
ba. 15.4.1770

Three children

Jane = William Rimmer
ba. 6.2.1780
m. 16.5.1802
ba. 8.7.1773
s. of Richard and Ellen

Ellen = John Pye
ba. F 21.1.1798
m. 17.7.1815
ba. 6.12.1795
s. of Miles and Mary

Richard = Priscilla Sawyer
ba. 19.12.1802
m. 24.7.1836
ba. 24.7.1808
d. of John and Margaret

Issue

Seven children

Margaret = John Marshall
ba. 5.4.1840
ba. CC 12.1.1840
s. of John and Jane

the hostess to the young visitors with whom this story began, for she and John took the farm after the Rimmers. Subsequently the old farm had to make way for the new property springing up in Arundel and Dunbar Roads. The last man known to have farmed at Common End was Aaron Carr, later a dairyman of Guildford Road.

25

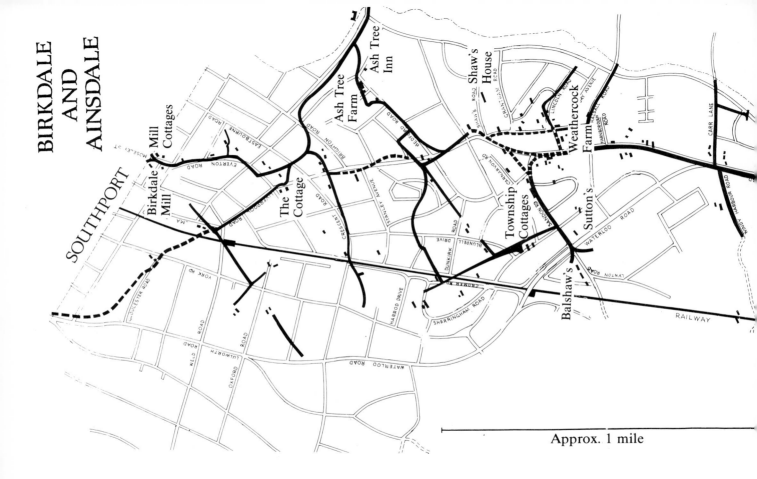

BIRKDALE
AND
AINSDALE

SOUTHPORT

Mill Cottages

Birkdale Mill

MOSELEY ST

EASTBOURNE ROAD

EVERTON ROAD

BRIGHTON ROAD

Ash Tree Farm

Ash Tree Inn

Shaw's House

SHAW'S ROAD

GRANTHAM ROAD

LINCOLN ROAD

HY AVENUE

Weathercock

Sutton's Farm

CARR LANE

The Cottage

CRESCENT ROAD

STANLEY AVENUE

BEDFORD ROAD

CARNARVON RD

SANDON ROAD

Township Cottages

BLUNDELL ROAD

DUNKIRK DRIVE

CROMER RD

HARROD DRIVE

SHERRINGHAM ROAD

WATERLOO ROAD

Balshaw's

WATERLOO ROAD

LYNTON ROAD

HARBOUR ROAD

RAILWAY

YORK RD

GLOUCESTER ROAD

WILD ROAD

OXFORD ROAD

LULWORTH ROAD

WATERLOO ROAD

Approx. 1 mile

26

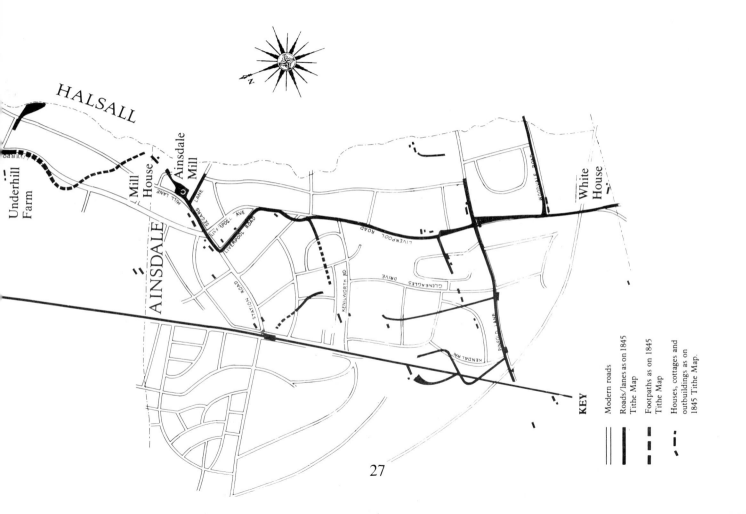

HALSALL

Underhill
Farm

Mill
House

AINSDALE

Ainsdale
Mill

MILL LANE

SECKERS LANE

FOOTPATH AVE

LIVERPOOL ROAD

STATION ROAD

KENILWORTH RD

GLENEAGLES DRIVE

PINFOLD LANE

KENDAL WAY

FOOTPATH MILL LANE

White
House

27

KEY

Modern roads

Roads/lanes as on 1845
Tithe Map

Footpaths as on 1845
Tithe Map

Houses, cottages and
outbuildings as on
1845 Tithe Map.

Balshaw's around the turn of the century.

Balshaw's, Birkdale

A popular ballad familiar to older people describes how 'weary and lame a boy there came up to the farmer's door'. The boy was seeking someone who would give him 'employ to plough and mow, to reap and sow, and be a farmer's boy'. This scene was enacted in real life in eighteenth-century Birkdale. The boy, Thomas Sawyer, was a runaway apprentice who could no longer endure life under his master in Preston. He had tramped southwards by unfrequented ways to avoid detection by the authorities who could have arrested him, finally travelling along the shore. Close to Birkdale he spotted amidst the sand-dunes a substantial, ancient farmstead. It was thatched and whitewashed, cruck-built and with two storeys at its eastern end, and was sheltered by a cop and a plantation of willows. In front was a fold and a large duck-pond. From the farm a lane ran inland, and along the lane were a smaller house and a cottage. The boy approached the farmhouse and asked for employment: he was kindly received, and offered work and accommodation, and the fact that he remained there permanently is a testimonial to both sides.

The farm belonged to the Balshaw family, William and his two sons, the younger of whom was already married. William senior died in 1742 leaving to Thomas, his elder son, the original farmhouse which his will described as 'my anchent old estate'. As the family first appears in the North Meols parish registers in 1595, this was probably an accurate description. To his other son, William, he left the 'new house and houseing adjoining' with two closes of ground lying at its east end, and an acre of meadow land. His daughters received financial bequests and Alice, the younger, was left in addition 'my little house of two bays'. Isabel, his wife, was left five pounds a year for life and a bed at her choice, with the furniture belonging to it, 'and to live with our daughter Alice in the little house at her pleasure'.

William Balshaw died within four years of his father, leaving a five-year-old daughter, Anne, and a one-month-old son, another William. He left no will, but his widow, Ellen, was appointed administratrix and an interesting inventory survives, showing that besides the usual farming and fishing gear, furniture, etc., he owned brass and pewter goods and a 'clock

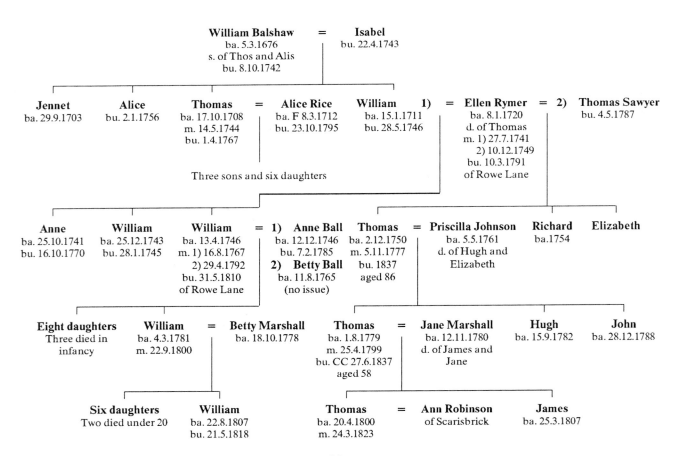

William Balshaw = Isabel
ba. 5.3.1676   bu. 22.4.1743
s. of Thos and Alis
bu. 8.10.1742

Jennet
ba. 29.9.1703

Alice
bu. 2.1.1756

Thomas = **Alice Rice**
ba. 17.10.1708   ba. F 8.3.1712
m. 14.5.1744   bu. 23.10.1795
bu. 1.4.1767

Three sons and six daughters

William 1) = **Ellen Rymer** = 2) **Thomas Sawyer**
ba. 15.1.1711   ba. 8.1.1720   bu. 4.5.1787
bu. 28.5.1746   d. of Thomas
m. 1) 27.7.1741
2) 10.12.1749
bu. 10.3.1791
of Rowe Lane

Anne
ba. 25.10.1741
bu. 16.10.1770

William
ba. 25.12.1743
bu. 28.1.1745

William = 1) **Anne Ball**
ba. 13.4.1746   ba. 12.12.1746
m. 1) 16.8.1767   bu. 7.2.1785
2) 29.4.1792   2) **Betty Ball**
bu. 31.5.1810   ba. 11.8.1765
of Rowe Lane   (no issue)

Thomas = **Priscilla Johnson**
ba. 2.12.1750   ba. 5.5.1761
m. 5.11.1777   d. of Hugh and
bu. 1837   Elizabeth
aged 86

Richard
ba.1754

Elizabeth

Eight daughters
Three died in
infancy

William = **Betty Marshall**
ba. 4.3.1781   ba. 18.10.1778
m. 22.9.1800

Thomas = **Jane Marshall**
ba. 1.8.1779   ba. 12.11.1780
m. 25.4.1799   d. of James and
bu. CC 27.6.1837   Jane
aged 58

Hugh
ba. 15.9.1782

John
ba. 28.12.1788

Six daughters
Two died under 20

William
ba. 22.8.1807
bu. 21.5.1818

Thomas = **Ann Robinson**
ba. 20.4.1800   of Scarisbrick
m. 24.3.1823

James
ba. 25.3.1807

30

and case'. Ellen was now running the farm, probably with the help of Thomas Sawyer, and it is not surprising that within another three years, in 1749, they were married. They had two sons, Thomas and Richard, and a daughter, Elizabeth, and all the Sawyers of 'old' Birkdale are their descendants.

Thomas senior obviously prospered, and took new opportunities when they arose. In 1761 he leased eleven acres of 'unimproved', that is undrained, land in Halsall at a low rental, with the intention of reclaiming the land and farming it. The other lives on the lease were Thomas' two sons, aged ten and seven, and his stepson William Balshaw, aged fifteen. When the three lives came to an end in 1837 on the death of Thomas Sawyer II at the great age of 86, he had long outlived his brother and stepbrother, and had enlarged his holding in Birkdale to over 46 acres.

There were still Balshaws in Birkdale up to 1820, but in that year the family seems to have died out, with the deaths of William Balshaw's grandchildren. No members of the family had lived in the ancestral home since 1795, when a yeoman described as 'Richard Rimmer black' took a lease on Balshaws. This was presumably the property owned by Thomas Balshaw, as 1795 was the year in which his widow Alice died, predeceased by all their three sons. The Balshaws appear to have become a sickly family by the eighteenth century.

In 1818 Richard Tomlinson, described as a taylor, took a seven-year lease on seven acres of Balshaws, which was presumably the part originally bequeathed to the younger brother, William. Names of farms, however, were often changed in this period with the advent of new owners, and the same name used for different farms over time. This can become very confusing. For example, since 1825 Thomas Sawyer III had been occupying property known as Carters, on the east side of what is now the Crescent Road railway crossing; but in 1832 he took a lease on Balshaws. Richard Rimmer had left his mark, for in that lease the property is called Rimmers. When Hugh Johnson, the school master, took the Birkdale census in 1841, however, he reverted to the time-honoured name of Balshaws – although the expanding Sawyer family lived in four of the five houses which are listed on the site!

Thomas III died within six months of his father, in 1837. By 1845 his son, Thomas IV, had removed to a farm in Southport. Family tradition has it that he moved because of his farm's proximity to the proposed new railway line between Southport and Liverpool. The line did not actually open until 1848, but surveying had been taking place since the early 1840s. Other members of the Sawyer family remained

Sketch of Balshaw's, by Cecil F. Rimmer.

in Birkdale, and the irony is that two of these, Hugh and James Sawyer, were in separate farms right on the new line.

By the 1861 census Peter Sawyer, cousin of Thomas, was the only householder actually of Balshaws: the satellite cottages were occupied by various families.

The last references known are in a street directory of 1934, where Balshaws Farm is given the address Lynton Road; and finally, a sad newspaper photograph (undated) showing the deliberate destruction by fire of this ancient farmstead.

Weathercock Farm.

Weathercock Farm, Birkdale

WEATHERCOCK Farm stood on the south-eastern perimeter of Birkdale Common, which was the centre of the township of Birkdale until the mid-nineteenth century. The ancient Moss Lane, mentioned in leases, was close by the farmhouse, merging with other lanes giving access to the north and to the south of Birkdale, and away to the Isle of Wight Farm and to Halsall.

In modern terms the farm would be sited on the south side of Norfolk Road, with an orchard towards Liverpool Road and a stack-yard towards Shaftesbury Road, the house lying between the two. It is possible that the building had two distinct phases in its history, being originally just a single-storey cottage, with a two-storey brick house added in the early years of the nineteenth century by the Blundells, who were in occupation by then.

Leases of the eighteenth century give some clues to finding the earlier occupiers. In the year 1730, reference was made in a lease to an area of land and to a dwelling, 'William Boond's Hey' and 'William Boond's Tenement', which coincided with the fields and farm which were later to be called Weathercock Farm. The Boond (Bond) family originated in Churchtown in The Rowe. The first one to come to Birkdale was a John Bond, whose entry in the North Meols register, with a nice attention to detail, tells that 'he was borne on December the 2nd about ten of the clock of the night and was baptized on December 6th, 1675'. Among John's many children was the above William who, in 1723, married Marjorie Balshaw at St. Cuthbert's Church. It seems likely that his tenancy of the farm would start about the time of his marriage; by the year 1737, however, the tenement had passed to the Marshall family, and they were to be closely connected with the farm for the rest of its history.

The Marshalls were one of the largest families in Birkdale, with many branches. Those at this farm became part of one of the most extraordinary events in Birkdale's history. John Marshall, who took over the farm in 1737, lost his wife, Margaret, two years later. Within six months of her death he had married Anne Sory, or Sawyer, 25 years old, eighteen years his junior, and already carrying his child. It was quite usual at this period for brides to be pregnant, since it was accepted as important that marriages should be fertile.

Anne had three sons. The unique baptism entry in

the North Meols register for her third son, James, reads as follows:

1746 ba. May 11. James s. of John Marshall of Birkdale & Anne his wife transported.

What had she done to deserve such a terrible sentence? The record of her trial at Lancaster Assizes states that she was convicted of stealing 22 shillings, and sentenced to seven years' transportation to the American colonies. As she was pregnant, the carrying out of the sentence was 'respited until after she was brought to bed'. What eventually happened to Anne is not known, but neither her husband nor her infant son appear to have suffered long-term consequences from her absence. John lived to be 91 and James, despite his unhappy start in life, surpassed even that, dying at the age of 92 in 1838. He had married first Ellen Bibby, daughter of the Ainsdale and Birkdale miller Joseph Bibby (thus introducing the unusual name of Joseph to the Marshall family), and had fourteen children by her and his second wife, Jane Rymer.

His eldest son, duly called Joseph after his maternal grandfather, became a shoemaker, and in 1801 leased half an acre on the east side of Little Common on which to build a three-bay house. He sold the family farm to the Blundells, who thus took over what had been known as Marshall's Tenement. If, as is likely, they extended the building, then a new, impressive name was required, and Weathercock House came into being.

The Blundells first appeared in Birkdale at the beginning of the eighteenth century and, particularly under the second Miles Blundell (1741–1823), soon established themselves in the area. Miles' growing importance is shown by the parish and manorial offices he held in the late eighteenth century. To name just a few, he was overseer, churchwarden, constable, burleyman, looker that no person keep more sheep than their fifteen, wreck-looker and haws-looker. By the early nineteenth century his elder son, James, was at Weathercock, and his younger son, John, farmed Charnleys and South End.

In 1819 the farm was associated with yet another scandal when, in February, John Blundell was murdered by Miles Blundell. John Blundell was the second cousin of James of Weathercock, but which Miles was the murderer? There were no fewer than seven Miles Blundells alive at that date, six of whom were old enough to commit the offence – including James' own son, and his nephew. The failure, even of the present-day descendants, to pin down the actual culprit indicates the difficulties of identifying people when names are so often repeated in families. That the

36

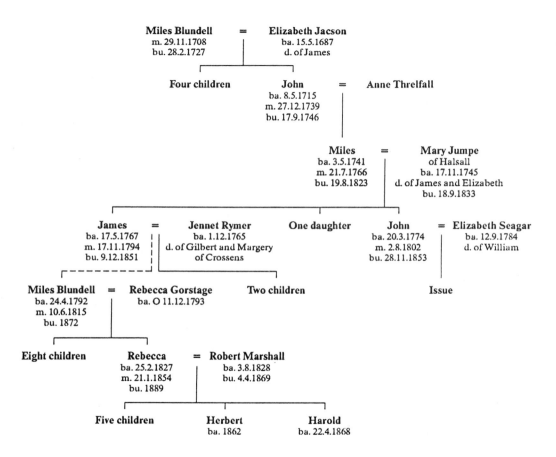

Miles Blundell　　=　　Elizabeth Jacson
m. 29.11.1708　　　　　ba. 15.5.1687
bu. 28.2.1727　　　　　　d. of James

Four children　　　John　　=　　Anne Threlfall
　　　　　　　　　　ba. 8.5.1715
　　　　　　　　　　m. 27.12.1739
　　　　　　　　　　bu. 17.9.1746

Miles　　=　　Mary Jumpe
ba. 3.5.1741　　　　of Halsall
m. 21.7.1766　　　　ba. 17.11.1745
bu. 19.8.1823　　　d. of James and Elizabeth
　　　　　　　　　　bu. 18.9.1833

James　　=　　Jennet Rymer　　One daughter　　John　　=　　Elizabeth Seagar
ba. 17.5.1767　　　ba. 1.12.1765　　　　　　　　　ba. 20.3.1774　　　ba. 12.9.1784
m. 17.11.1794　　d. of Gilbert and Margery　　　m. 2.8.1802　　　d. of William
bu. 9.12.1851　　of Crossens　　　　　　　　　　bu. 28.11.1853

Miles Blundell　=　Rebecca Gorstage　　Two children　　　　Issue
ba. 24.4.1792　　ba. O 11.12.1793
m. 10.6.1815
bu. 1872

Eight children　　Rebecca　　=　　Robert Marshall
　　　　　　　　ba. 25.2.1827　　　ba. 3.8.1828
　　　　　　　　m. 21.1.1854　　　bu. 4.4.1869
　　　　　　　　bu. 1889

Five children　　Herbert　　　Harold
　　　　　　　ba. 1862　　　ba. 22.4.1868

37

Horses on the West Heys.

38

whole event was sorted out within the family is indicated by the fact that the murderer does not appear to have gone for trial.

James' son Miles married Rebecca Gorstage in 1814, and by the 1841 census was living at Weathercock with six of his children, plus a daughter-in-law and a niece, Ellen Gorstage. In the 1851 census James, now 83, was living with them: he died soon afterwards. Miles died in 1872, aged 80, and it is interesting that it was his son-in-law, Robert Marshall, who helped him run the farm and whose family then took it over. Thus the Marshalls, albeit a different branch from that of the eighteenth century, were back on the land.

The extent of the farm by 1861 was 51 acres of mixed arable and grazing land, with three men employed. Robert Marshall died young, but fortunately his widow, another Rebecca, successfully carried on the role of her husband and continued to manage the farm. Herbert, her son, followed on in her footsteps until 1906, when the farmhouse was vacated and probably demolished in the same year. Harold Marshall, her youngest son, rented the fields known as the West Heys and carried on working as a milk dealer until his death. The fact that Dunbar Crescent is built on the site of these fields gives an idea of the extent of Weathercock Farm, which formed the background to the lives of the generations of occupants of Weathercock House.

Underhill Farm in the 1890s.

Underhill Farm, Birkdale

THE name 'Underhill' has become attached to several farms because of their situation, but to none more aptly than this, nestling as it did beside a great sandhill which dominated the road to Ainsdale. Older local residents may remember it, looming above the road opposite the Farm School (now St. Thomas More's), and in its later days being shored up by railway sleepers. In the early 1920s a team of Irish labourers was employed to remove the sandhill, being sustained throughout with drinks from the farm.

It was a Rimmer farm through the eighteenth and most of the nineteenth centuries, and was distinguished from other Rimmer and Underhill farms by the name Latham Rimmer Underhill Farm. By the early twentieth century it was farmed by the Berry family who, having been obliged to leave a farm in Nelson for a place more suited to an invalid son, found at Underhill exactly what was required. The air proved beneficial and the land, although not rich enough to grow corn or oats, supported a full range of vegetables for sale and for their own use, as well as pasturing their sixteen cows and their gentle Friesian bull for a thriving dairy business. Father and children sold milk as far afield as Aughton Road by various means of transport, from a milk-float to cans hung on the handlebars of a bicycle. A large barn sheltered the cattle and horses, with a hay loft above, and other buildings housed pigs, ducks and chickens.

Farmer Berry was a highly respected man who, although having interests outside the farm, always had such concern for his animals that he would never leave the farm in the evening without ensuring that every single one was under cover. Even the aggressive cow which tossed him into a ditch one day; the horse that ran wild in the sandhills, refusing to be tamed to do any useful work; and the nervous goat that would hide under a table when the cows arrived for milking – all were equally cherished and had their place in the life of the farm.

The fields of the farm lay from north of the Birkdale Cemetery to Windy Harbour Road. A five-barred gate and rutted cart track, hawthorn-hedged, gave access from Liverpool Road. The point of entry opposite Nixons Lane now leads to a recreation ground. This area was one naturally rich in plant and animal life, and already in 1903 when there was a meeting of the

British Association in Southport, an article was written bemoaning the loss of certain rare plants of the locality because of 'the advance of civilization'. Many varieties of wild flowers and plants were to be seen, lizards also abounded, and there was a stream which, in addition to the beauty of its marsh-marigolds, forget-me-nots and rushes, provided wild mint and watercress. Nettles were harvested for Mrs. Berry's nettle beer, and mushrooms picked from certain fields were a source of income for the children, who would be allowed to keep the proceeds of their sale if they would be up at dawn to collect them. Blackberries from the hedges added to the variety of fruits from the orchard, to keep the larder well stocked for baking.

The Berrys had another pride and joy on the farm. They owned amongst their farm vehicles a trap with beautifully panelled and polished coachwork, which had been destined for an owner in the diamond mines of South Africa but, because of the war, became available – a frustrated export of its day! The nearest public transport was the tram from the Crown Hotel.

The house was long, single-storeyed, thatched and with the traditional whitewashed daub-covered walls. A rail fence gave some privacy from the rest of the farm. Flagged floors were brightened by rag rugs made by Mr. Berry, and white madras curtains hung at the cottage windows. Keeping the oil lamps in good trim was a lengthy process, with the one in the parlour being a particularly elaborate style compared with the other rooms.

Cottage life had its inevitable discomforts, but these were accepted philosophically. There was piped water to the scullery, which was completely separate from the house, so entailing a trip outdoors to do the washing up, or carrying water back and forth. The well water was used for the stock. A primitive one-hole privy was some thirty yards from the house and, as nervous individuals liked to have a companion on a dark night, an improvised shelter was made by kind Mr. Berry as a protection from the weather while waiting one's turn!

The annual visit to Ince Blundell Hall to pay the rent was (perhaps surprisingly) anticipated with pleasure. The day had a holiday atmosphere, with a meal provided in a tent on the lawn. Several couples joined together to hire a taxi for the journey.

The immediate predecessors of the Berry family at Underhill were of the Todd family, but prior to that the Rimmer name predominates. In the census years of 1841 and 1851 Richard Rimmer and his wife Ellen (also a Rimmer) and their family farmed eighty acres, with the help of four agricultural labourers, a nephew,

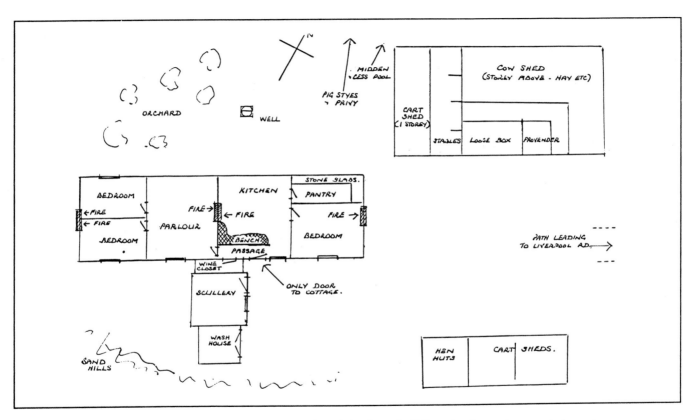

Underhill Farm: an impression (not to scale) of the farm buildings in the early twentieth century.

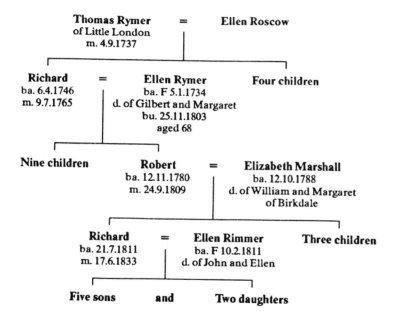

Thomas Rymer
of Little London
m. 4.9.1737

=

Ellen Roscow

Richard
ba. 6.4.1746
m. 9.7.1765

=

Ellen Rymer
ba. F 5.1.1734
d. of Gilbert and Margaret
bu. 25.11.1803
aged 68

Four children

Nine children

Robert
ba. 12.11.1780
m. 24.9.1809

=

Elizabeth Marshall
ba. 12.10.1788
d. of William and Margaret
of Birkdale

Richard
ba. 21.7.1811
m. 17.6.1833

=

Ellen Rimmer
ba. F 10.2.1811
d. of John and Ellen

Three children

Five sons   **and**   **Two daughters**

who was the servant, and Ellen's father, John. Richard's father, Robert, was the tenth child of another Richard and Ellen Rimmer (again, Ellen's maiden name was Rimmer).

Later in the century another Rimmer family appeared in the records. This was James and Alice, who had been living in Scarisbrick, where four of their children were born; but the fifth child, George, was born in Birkdale – presumably at Underhill, or 'Dicks' as it was known then (whether from one of the Richards mentioned above, or from bygone generations, is not known). George later carried on the farming tradition at South End Farm.

The 1920s and 1930s saw the gradual nibbling away of the farm fields to satisfy the need for more recreation grounds, more cemetery space, more housing and, eventually, a school. Finally, the cottage of Underhill and its neighbour, Windy Harbour Farm Cottage, lay empty for a while before disappearing from the scene.

Ainsdale Mill and Millhouse Farm

MOST villages had a mill, owned by the lord of the manor, where tenants had to grind their corn – with severe penalties for disobedience. So it was in Birkdale and Ainsdale. Local leases granted by the Blundells of Ince, lords of both manors, almost invariably contained a clause requiring the lessee to grind his corn at the lord's mill, and forbidding him to set up 'any querne, handmill or horse mill'. (Occasionally there was a proviso: 'unless it be in time of necessity when the said mill cannot grind for want of wind'.) Failure to comply could lead even to the termination of the lease, demonstrating clearly that the charges for milling formed a valuable part of the lord's revenue.

The first reference to a mill in Ainsdale is in a lease to Richard Rimmer of Birkdale, 'commonly called Black Dick', in 1631. The phraseology of the lease, 'the now windmill', suggests that the mill had been recently installed. As Robert Blundell had just acquired the manors of Birkdale and Ainsdale from the Halsalls of Halsall, he may have erected his windmill to capture the profits which would formerly have gone to the mill at Halsall. He caused the new building to be situated very close to the boundary between Ainsdale and Birkdale since, until the middle of the eighteenth century, it served both settlements. The same lease states that the mill is 'in the possession of Cuthbert Rimmer', so presumably he was the first miller at Ainsdale, and the first in a long line of Rimmers connected with the mill and millhouse.

The early mill was not the brick-built tower-mill still remembered in its decapitated form by many local people. It was probably a wooden building more like the one erected in Birkdale 150 years later. Jane Eddington, writing in the 1890s, says that her great-grandfather 'built Ainsdale mill and the Millhouse'. He was John Rimmer, born in 1739, died 1821, so his mill was probably built in the late eighteenth century. He was, according to Jane, 'very prosperous and good and noble in all his dealings. He had money and he speculated in trade and made a lot more money'. She lists the property he owned, not only in Ainsdale, but in Lathom, Leyland and Liverpool; and ranging from cottages and farms in Ainsdale, Birkdale and Rowe Lane, to a public house and a shoe shop in Liverpool.

Various millers are listed as 'of Ainsdale', but the

Ainsdale Windmill, by G. Harrison.

46

one certain to be known to posterity is William Dickinson, for it was he who became the census enumerator in 1841: probably not an arduous task, as there were only 35 houses, three of which were uninhabited. William was born in Formby in 1803 and married in 1828, when he was a school master. His wife was Catherine Rimmer, born in Birkdale in 1807, but described in the marriage register as 'of Ormskirk'. They were at Ainsdale mill in 1832, William having resigned as Formby school master over non-payment of his salary. They were still there when the 1851 census was taken, so they had a long stay, during which they raised a large family.

Some time in the 1880s or earlier, the mill was taken over by a family named Collier, wind-power was no longer used, and the tower-mill began its decline into ruin. The last owner, a great-nephew of the Colliers, applied to have it listed, but this was refused. Local vandals made the structure dangerous, and in 1970 it was demolished in the interests of safety.

A feature still remembered in the later years of the mill was the railway which ran to it from Ainsdale station siding, carrying grain, groundnuts from West Africa, soya beans and other items brought up the line from Liverpool docks. There was an incline from Ainsdale station down to the mill and the loaded wagons travelled by gravity, controlled by a brakes-man. On the return journey the empty wagons were propelled by an engine. To allow the passage of the train, a huge hinged gate closed Liverpool Road to traffic at a point opposite Ainsdale Laundry, just north of what is now Burnley Road.

The mill and Millhouse Farm seem to have passed into divided ownership in the eighteenth century. While millers of various names are listed as 'of Ainsdale', the farm seems to have remained in a branch of the Rimmer family, and some of the older residents of Ainsdale still remember the farmhouse and its last occupants. They were two elderly sisters, Kitty, born in 1845, and Ellen, born in 1847. The youngest children of Thomas Rimmer, the blacksmith, and his wife Catherine Eccles, who earlier lived at Black Hall Farm, they were descendants of Richard Rimmer 'de Mill', a relation of John Rimmer, the builder of the mill and mill house. They are remembered by their great-niece as two quaint figures carrying their home-produced butter to Ainsdale station in large, shallow baskets, on their way to Liverpool market. Around the farm they wore 'farm bonnets' and long skirts. 'Old Kitty', as she was disrespectfully known, was the terror of small boys in the 1920s. They used to trespass on 'Kitty's Hills' or steal apples from her orchard, until scattered by the warning cry, 'Kitty's coming!'.

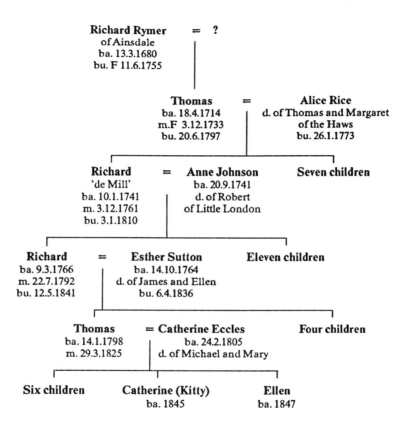

Richard Rymer = ?
of Ainsdale
ba. 13.3.1680
bu. F 11.6.1755

Thomas = Alice Rice
ba. 18.4.1714　　　d. of Thomas and Margaret
m.F 3.12.1733　　　of the Haws
bu. 20.6.1797　　　bu. 26.1.1773

Richard = Anne Johnson　　Seven children
'de Mill'　　ba. 20.9.1741
ba. 10.1.1741　d. of Robert
m. 3.12.1761　of Little London
bu. 3.1.1810

Richard = Esther Sutton　　Eleven children
ba. 9.3.1766　　ba. 14.10.1764
m. 22.7.1792　　d. of James and Ellen
bu. 12.5.1841　　bu. 6.4.1836

Thomas = Catherine Eccles　　Four children
ba. 14.1.1798　　ba. 24.2.1805
m. 29.3.1825　　d. of Michael and Mary

Six children　　Catherine (Kitty)　　Ellen
　　　　　　　　ba. 1845　　　　ba. 1847

48

Old Mill from Mill Lane, Ainsdale.

It seems from the evidence that the farmhouse, like the mill, was rebuilt in brick by John Rimmer, Jane Eddington's great-grandfather, on the same or a very similar ground-plan to its predecessor. It stood in what is now Oakwood Avenue and faced north towards Birkdale. It was on two floors except at its eastern end, where the roof came down over a projecting one-storey section. At the western end a flight of external stone steps led to a store-room, which in earlier times had probably been a sleeping loft with access from within the house. The inside walls of the house were whitewashed and the ground floors flagged; the centre of the kitchen floor was sanded and the surround stoned. Access to the upper floor was by a stairway more like a ladder.

Opposite the house, but slightly to the side, was the barn which was similarly of brick, with a slate roof and massive doors. Between the house and barn was an area of green grass kept close-cropped by the pony belonging to the local fish purveyor, which was stabled in Kitty's barn. About three yards from the back door was the covered well from which water was obtained by a 'piggon' – a long pole on the end of which was a bucket arrangement. The house was surrounded by trees: to the east an orchard growing apples, pears, plums and damsons, and to the west a cop five feet high with trees growing upon it.

White House Farm, Ainsdale.

White House Farm, Ainsdale

THE White House still straddles the Ainsdale–Formby border as it has done for centuries, though it is much altered externally. Although right on the doorstep of the Formby Hall estate, the house and land belonged to the Blundells of Ince Blundell, being part of their manor of Ainsdale. Ainsdale and Formby were linked for ecclesiastical purposes, since Ainsdale was in the Chapelry of Formby which was a 'detached' part of the parish of Walton-on-the-Hill, Liverpool, 'detached' meaning that it was separated from Walton by other parishes. From 1746 baptisms, marriages and burials of Ainsdale folk took place at the new church of St. Peter's, Formby, which was built to replace the old parish church finally destroyed by a great storm in 1739.

The early history of the house is not well documented, but from a lease of 1787 we know that the building consisted of 'a dwelling house and kitchen containing four bays and outhousing eleven bays'. Since a bay was normally between twelve and fifteen feet wide, this was a farmstead of considerable size, and by far the largest in Ainsdale. The long outbuildings lay to the west of the house, facing south-west. There were nearly sixteen acres of land: an orchard by the house, then the North Hey, Little Acre and Big Acre in Ainsdale; and South Hey and Green over the boundary in Formby.

The lessee in 1787 was Elizabeth Marrow (née Rimmer), widow of Robert Marrow, a broker of Liverpool, and the three lives in the lease were their three daughters, Elizabeth, Mary and Nanny, aged ten, eight and six years. A note added to the document states that 'Mr. Blundell agreed to add Mrs. Marrow's life in the room of her daughter Nanny Marrow who at the date of the within deed was ill of a fever in case she died in the two months next ensuing'. Nanny, however, survived, evidently outliving her sisters, as another note says that 'this lease ceased on the Death of Nanny Marrow 22 October 1857'. She would then be aged 76. She is presumably the Miss Marrow recorded in the estate accounts as paying an annual rent of £3 3s. 0d. in 1841, which was the same amount agreed by her mother 54 years earlier!

The conditions of this lease make interesting reading. Mrs. Marrow was required to grind her corn at either Ainsdale or Formby Mill, and to plant starr

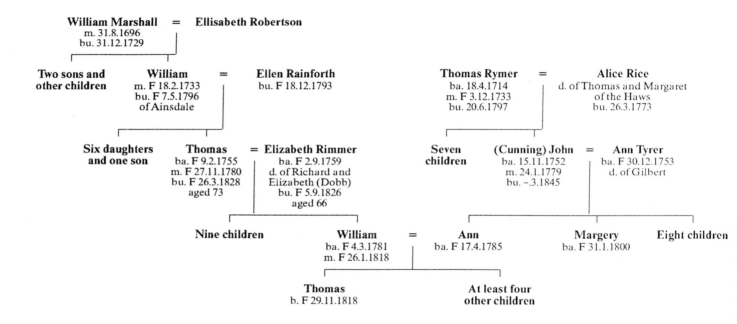

William Marshall = **Ellisabeth Robertson**
m. 31.8.1696
bu. 31.12.1729

Two sons and other children   **William** = **Ellen Rainforth**
m. F 18.2.1733   bu. F 18.12.1793
bu. F 7.5.1796
of Ainsdale

Thomas Rymer = **Alice Rice**
ba. 18.4.1714   d. of Thomas and Margaret
m. F 3.12.1733   of the Haws
bu. 20.6.1797   bu. 26.3.1773

Six daughters and one son   **Thomas** = **Elizabeth Rimmer**
ba. F 9.2.1755   ba. F 2.9.1759
m. F 27.11.1780   d. of Richard and
bu. F 26.3.1828   Elizabeth (Dobb)
aged 73   bu. F 5.9.1826
aged 66

Seven children   **(Cunning) John** = **Ann Tyrer**
ba. 15.11.1752   ba. F 30.12.1753
m. 24.1.1779   d. of Gilbert
bu. -.3.1845

Nine children   **William** = **Ann**
ba. F 4.3.1781   ba. F 17.4.1785
m. F 26.1.1818

Margery   **Eight children**
ba. F 31.1.1800

Thomas   **At least four**
b. F 29.11.1818   **other children**

grass or bent 'upon such sandhills as Henry Blundell . . . shall appoint'. She was not to take game or rabbits and, furthermore, was to inform Henry Blundell if she knew of anyone doing so without permission. She had to keep a dog and a cock for the use of the Lord of the Manor. Towards the end of the lease when only one life remained in being, there were also strict controls on how much land could be ploughed, with very heavy penalties of £10 per annum per acre if it was ploughed contrary to the terms of the lease.

Though Elizabeth Marrow and the other 'lives' held the lease of the White House, and were responsible for the above conditions being observed, they never lived there. In 1787 it was occupied by Thomas Marshall, his wife Elizabeth, and their four young sons. Their family eventually numbered ten; six sons and four daughters. With such a large family to maintain, it is not surprising that in 1806 Thomas, described as 'yeoman', took out a lease on his own account for a further three acres of land in Formby, next to that which he already rented from Mrs. Marrow. He was still required to plant starr grass to stabilise the dunes, and was also required to plant trees each year: either three full trees such as oak or ash, or one hundred hawthorn. He paid annually for these three acres the same sum, three guineas, as Mrs. Marrow had paid for five times as much land nineteen years before. The Marshalls' next neighbour to the north was John Rimmer, one of the sons of Thomas and Alice of Ainsdale Mill. He had acquired the nickname of 'Cunning John', for a field on the farm next to his is described as 'Field facing Cunning Johns'. John and his wife, Ann Tyrer, also had a large family of ten children, this time four sons and six daughters. Despite what would seem to be a good opportunity, there is evidence of only one intermarriage. Thomas' eldest son, William, married John's third daughter, Ann. 'Cunning John' lived to be about ninety, and his youngest daughter, Margery, who was unmarried, eventually took over the farm. Her nephew, another Thomas Marshall, son of William and Ann, was resident there at the time of the 1851 census, presumably to help her.

The position of the White House, right across the Ainsdale–Formby boundary, obviously confused the 1851 census enumerators since, though the farmhouse was and still is definitely in Ainsdale, it was not included in the Ainsdale returns. This may be because, by the time of the tithe apportionments of the mid-1840s, the farmer, William Marshall, held more land in Formby (twenty acres) than in Ainsdale (sixteen acres – as in the 1787 lease).

By about 1876 the Marshalls had left, and a family named Abram moved in from Lydiate to farm there. One of their descendants remembers an old family joke referring to the position of the White House, poised across the boundary: 'They bathed the baby in Formby and dried him in Ainsdale'.

Glossary

Bay: the space between two crucks or party-walls of a structure, usually between twelve and fifteen feet wide.

Cop: a high sandhill or a bank of mud or sods enclosing a field.

Down-dub: a lean-to, or single-storey addition at the end of a main structure used, for example, for a kitchen or privy.

Firehouse: the main living-room of a house, often the only room with a fireplace and open to the roof.

Fishing-stalls: sections of the shore, marked out and leased from the lord of the manor.

Gorstile: a piece of land on the eastern boundary of Birkdale, divided into narrow strips, each held by a different tenant.

Hawes: sandhills.

Hey: an enclosure or field.

Inventory: valuation of a person's goods made after death.

Leases with Lives: up to the nineteenth century, new leases were usually granted for the length of three named lives.

Starr or bent: marram grass, essential to the stabilising of the sand dunes.

Warren: specially farmed and managed rabbit warrens on the sand dunes.

Wham: wet or boggy land, prized in Birkdale, where most land was basically sand.

Yeoman: a substantial farmer, below the level of the gentry.